SandCastle™
Mini Animal Marvels

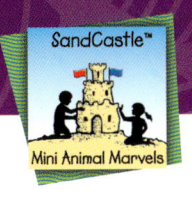

Miniature Dogs

A Division of ABDO
ABDO Publishing Company

Alex Kuskowski Consulting Editor, Diane Craig, M.A./Reading Specialist

visit us at www.abdopublishing.com

Published by ABDO Publishing Company, a division of ABDO, P.O. Box 398166, Minneapolis, Minnesota 55439. Copyright © 2014 by Abdo Consulting Group, Inc. International copyrights reserved in all countries. No part of this book may be reproduced in any form without written permission from the publisher. SandCastle™ is a trademark and logo of ABDO Publishing Company.

Printed in the United States of America, North Mankato, Minnesota
102013
012014

PRINTED ON RECYCLED PAPER

Editor: Liz Salzmann
Content Developer: Alex Kuskowski
Cover and Interior Design and Production: Mighty Media, Inc.
Photo Credits: Shutterstock

Library of Congress Cataloging-in-Publication Data

Kuskowski, Alex.
  Miniature dogs / Alex Kuskowski.
    pages cm. -- (Mini animal marvels)
  ISBN 978-1-62403-065-9
  1. Dogs--Juvenile literature. 2. Dogs--Size--Juvenile literature. I. Title.
  SF426.5.K87 2014
  636.76--dc23
                              2013022902

SandCastle™ Level: Transitional

SandCastle™ books are created by a team of professional educators, reading specialists, and content developers around five essential components—phonemic awareness, phonics, vocabulary, text comprehension, and fluency—to assist young readers as they develop reading skills and strategies and increase their general knowledge. All books are written, reviewed, and leveled for guided reading, early reading intervention, and Accelerated Reader® programs for use in shared, guided, and independent reading and writing activities to support a balanced approach to literacy instruction. The SandCastle™ series has four levels that correspond to early literacy development. The levels are provided to help teachers and parents select appropriate books for young readers.

Emerging Readers (no flags)   Beginning Readers (1 flag)   Transitional Readers (2 flags)   Fluent Readers (3 flags)

Table of Contents

Miniature Dogs 4
Toy Poodle 6
Miniature Pinscher 10
Miniature Schnauzer 14
Alaskan Klee Kai 18
Did You Know? 22
Dog Quiz 23
Glossary 24

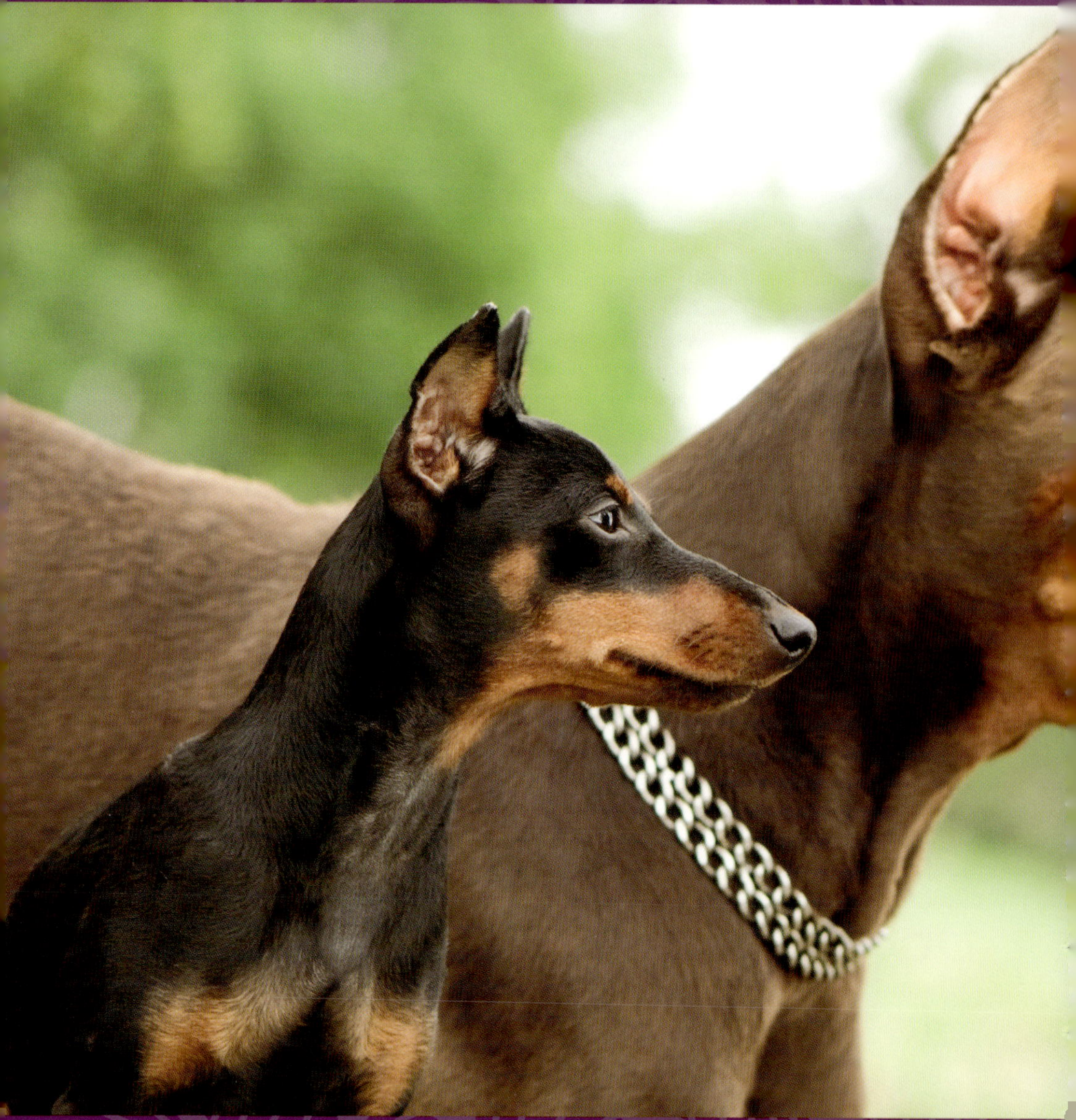

Miniature Dogs

Miniature dogs are small. They look like smaller **versions** of bigger dogs.

Toy Poodle

The toy poodle is a small poodle. It is a smart dog. It is easy to train.

6 feet (1.8 m)

It is 10 inches (25.4 cm) tall.

10 inches (25.4 cm)

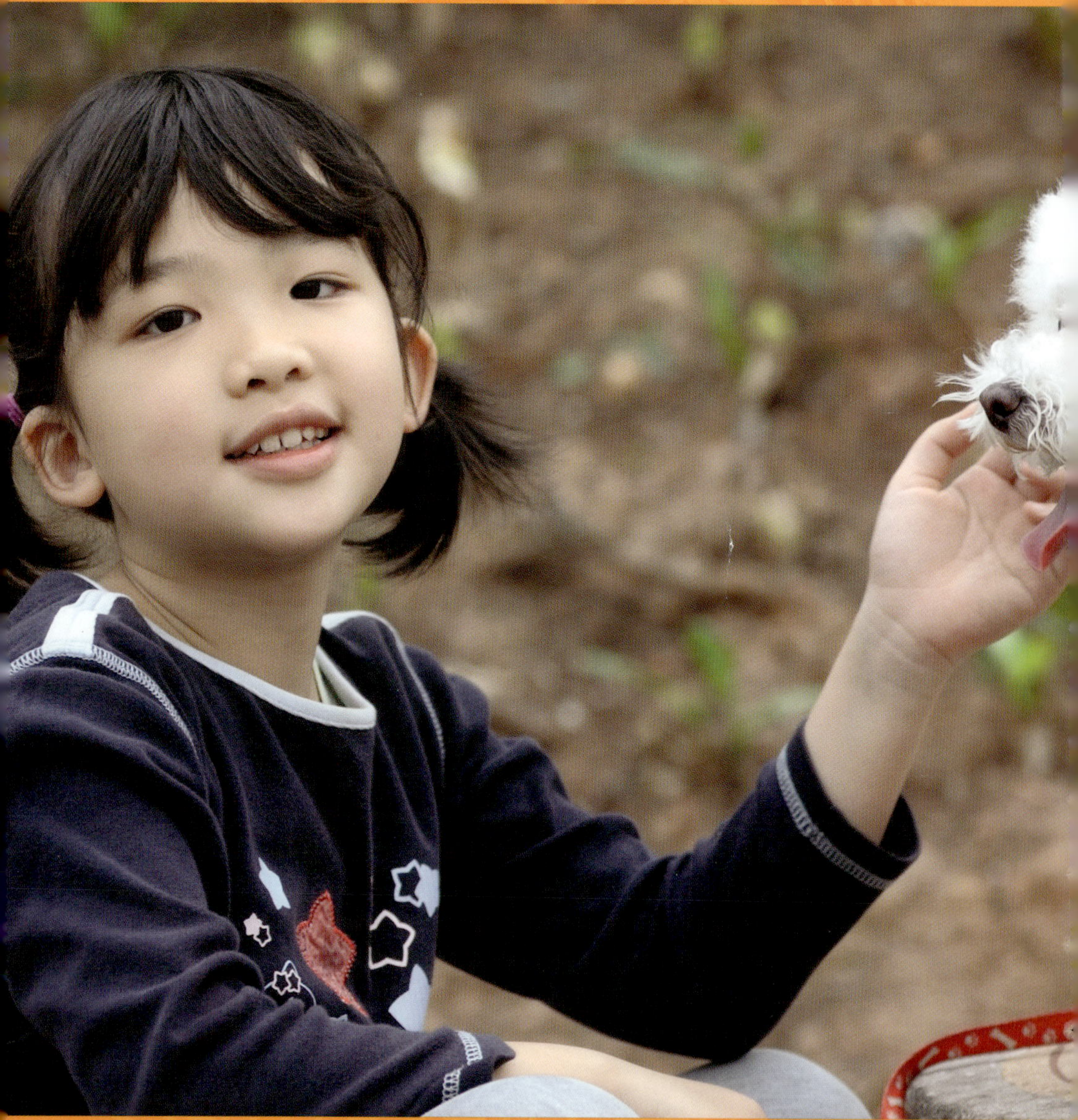

Toy poodles learn fast. They love to show off. Many people teach their toy poodles to do tricks.

Miniature Pinscher

Mini pinschers look like small Dobermans. They are **energetic**. They play outside.

6 feet
(1.8 m)

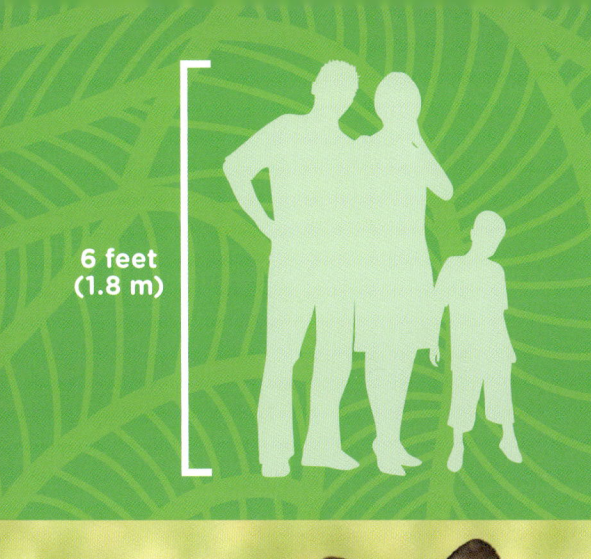

It is 12 inches (30.5 cm) tall.

12 inches
(30.5 cm)

11

Mini pinschers make good watchdogs.

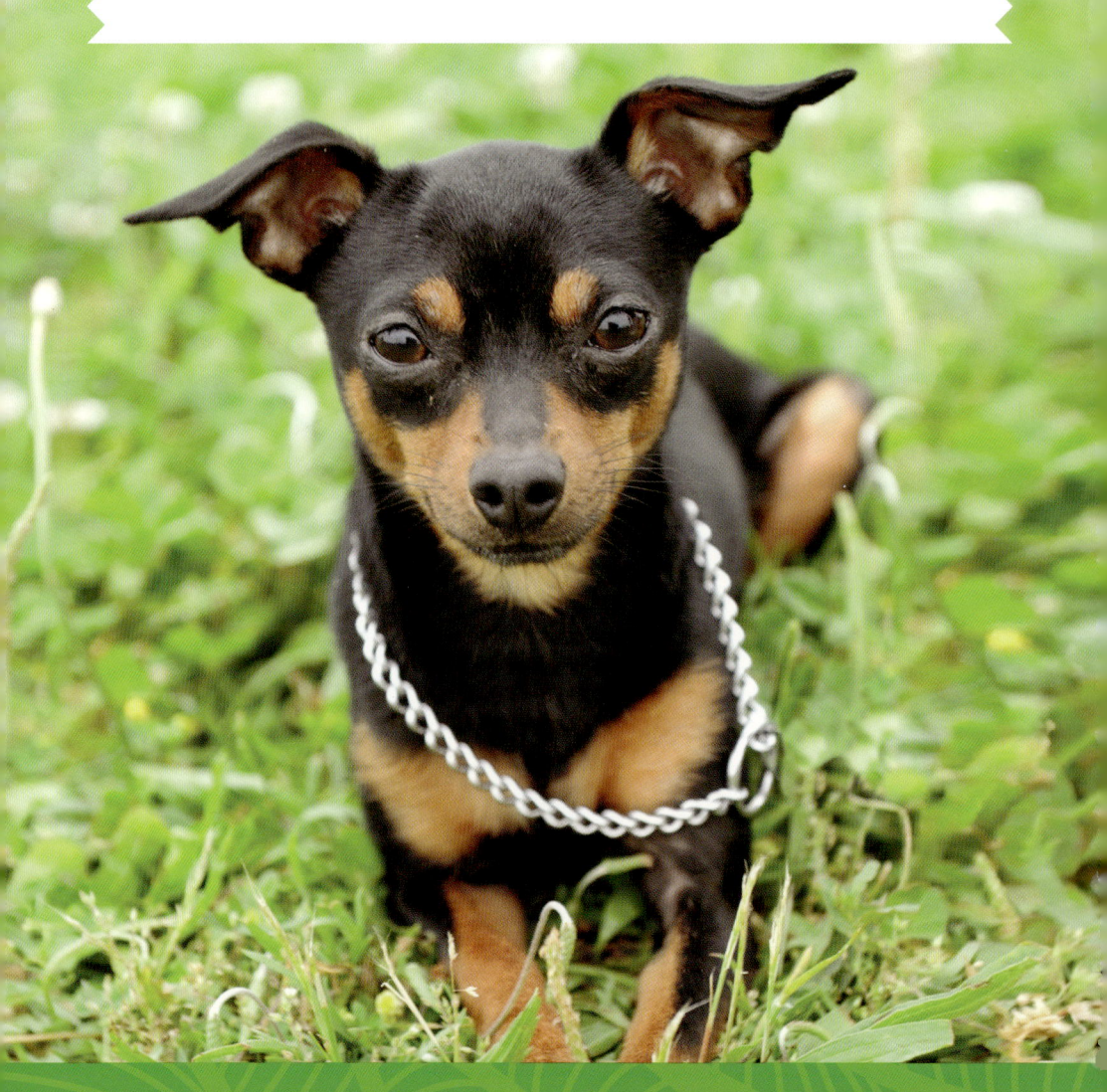

The mini pinscher's **nickname** is "King of the Toys."

13

Miniature Schnauzer

The mini schnauzer is small. It has a big bark. It barks when it is happy or afraid.

6 feet
(1.8 m)

It is 14 inches (35.6 cm) tall.

14 inches (35.6 cm)

15

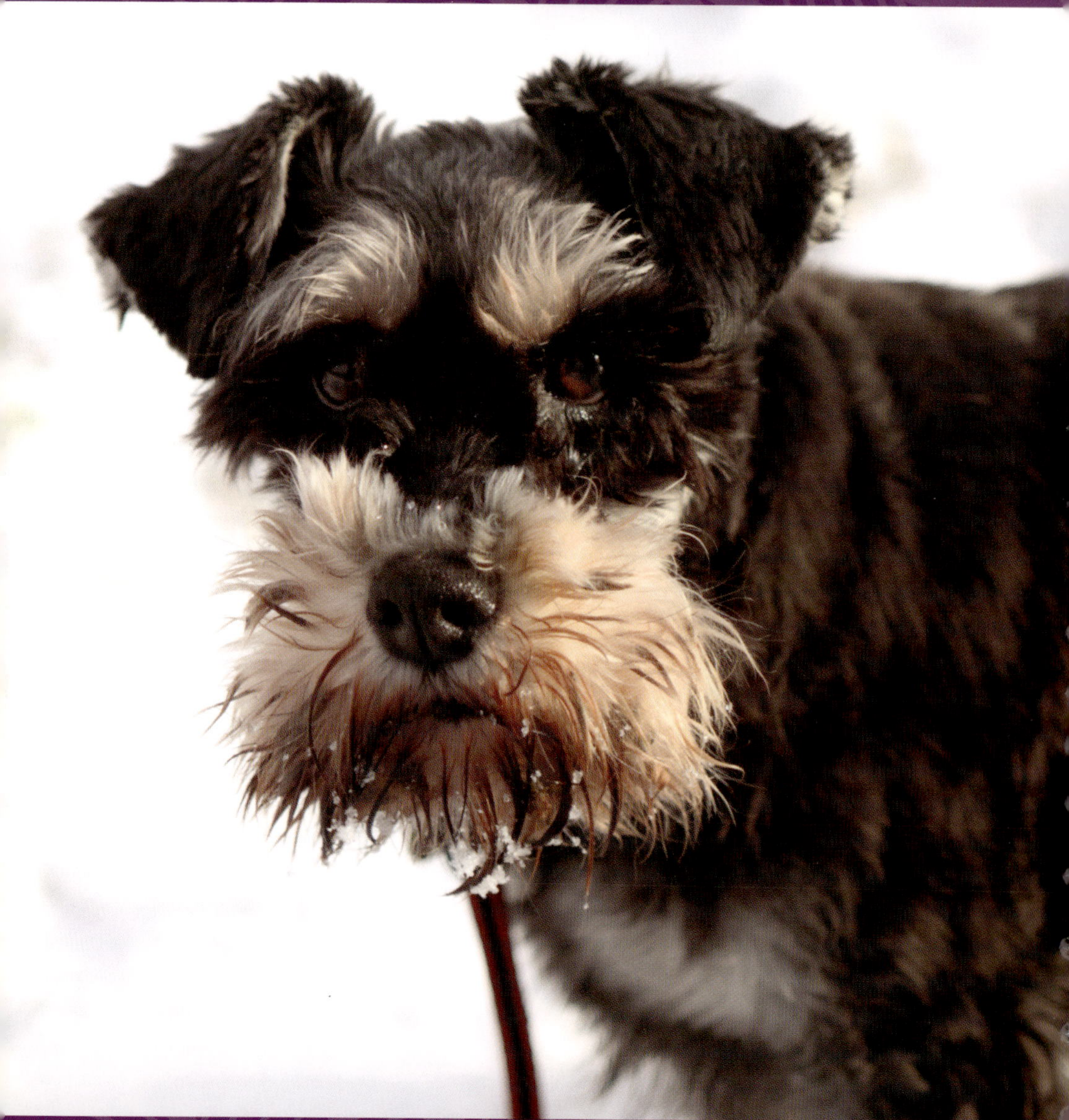

The mini schnauzer has a thick coat. The coat has two **layers** of fur. This keeps the dog warm.

Alaskan Klee Kai

The Alaskan klee kai looks like a mini husky. Klee kai means "small dog" in Athabaskan.

6 feet (1.8 m)

It is 15 inches (38.1 cm) tall.

15 inches (38.1 cm)

The Alaskan klee kai is active. It needs exercise every day.

The Alaskan klee kai is curious. It likes to **explore**.

Did You Know?

- Toy poodles live longer than standard poodles.

- The miniature pinscher has a short coat.

- Schnauzers came from Germany in the 1800s.

- There are three sizes of Alaskan klee kai.

Dog Quiz

1. Toy poodles learn slowly.

2. Mini pinschers are not good watchdogs.

3. The mini pinscher doesn't have a **nickname**.

4. The mini schnauzer has two **layers** of fur.

5. The Alaskan klee kai is smaller than the Alaskan husky.

Answers: 1. False 2. False 3. False 4. True 5. True

Glossary

energetic – active and full of energy.

explore – to move around an area to see what's there.

layer – one thickness of something that may be over or under another thickness.

nickname – a name given to someone or something in addition to the real name.

version – a different form or type from the original.